I'm Going To READ!™

These levels are meant only as guides;
you and your child can best choose a book that's right.

Level 1: Kindergarten–Grade 1 . . . Ages 4–6

- word bank to highlight new words
- consistent placement of text to promote readability
- easy words and phrases
- simple sentences build to make simple stories
- art and design help new readers decode text

Level 2: Grade 1 . . . Ages 6–7

- word bank to highlight new words
- rhyming texts introduced
- more difficult words, but vocabulary is still limited
- longer sentences and longer stories
- designed for easy readability

Level 3: Grade 2 . . . Ages 7–8

- richer vocabulary of up to 200 different words
- varied sentence structure
- high-interest stories with longer plots
- designed to promote independent reading

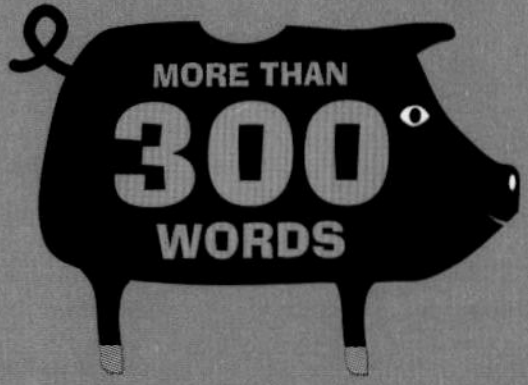

Level 4: Grades 3 and up . . . Ages 8 and up

- richer vocabulary of more than 300 different words
- short chapters, multi
- more complex plots ader
- emphasis on readin

LEVEL 3

Library of Congress Cataloging-in-Publication Data Available

2 4 6 8 10 9 7 5 3 1

Published by Sterling Publishing Co., Inc.
387 Park Avenue South, New York, NY 10016
Text copyright © 2005 by Harriet Ziefert Inc.
Illustrations copyright © 2005 by Rick Brown
Distributed in Canada by Sterling Publishing
c/o Canadian Manda Group, 165 Dufferin Street
Toronto, Ontario, Canada M6K 3H6
Distributed in Great Britain and Europe by Chris Lloyd at Orca Book
Services, Stanley House, Fleets Lane, Poole BH15 3AJ, England
Distributed in Australia by Capricorn Link (Australia) Pty. Ltd.
P.O. Box 704, Windsor, NSW 2756, Australia

I'm Going To Read is a trademark of Sterling Publishing Co., Inc.

Sterling ISBN 1-4027-2109-9

GOOD LUCK, BAD LUCK

Pictures by Rick Brown

Sterling Publishing Co., Inc.
New York

It's good luck
to throw a shoe
over your shoulder.

It's bad luck
to break
a shoelace.

One shoe off
and one shoe on—

that can
also bring
bad luck.

For good luck
on the way
to school—

step on every
crack in the
sidewalk or . . .

DON'T
step on any!

It's bad luck
if a black cat
crosses your path,
unless—

you cross
your arms
and fingers
and toes . . .

or roll up
your pants . . .

or take nine
steps backward!

If the first robin
you see in spring flies up,

you will have
good luck
for the rest
of the year.

But if it flies down . . .
you
won't.

Sprinkle salt on the tail of a bird.
You might have good luck.

It's good luck when
a spider swings down
in front of you.

And it's very, *very* lucky
to find the first letter
of your name in a web.

BUT . . .

stepping on
a spider can
bring bad luck.

Walking under
a ladder can too.

It's good luck
to catch a falling
leaf.

It's also good luck to
find a four-leaf clover.

Three and **seven**
are lucky numbers.

But **thirteen** can mean bad luck.

It's lucky to see
the new moon
over your shoulder.

Make a wish
and maybe
it will come true.

Wish on the first star you see tonight:

Star light, star bright,
The first star I see tonight.
I wish I may, I wish I might
Get the wish I wish tonight.